I0489123

Flower Mandala Coloring Book for Relaxation

Relaxing Art – Flower Mandalas Coloring Book

Flower Mandala

By : Gala Publication

Published By :

Gala Publication
© Copyright 2015 – Gala Publication

ISBN-13: **978-1522722151**
ISBN-10: **1522722157**

Design 1

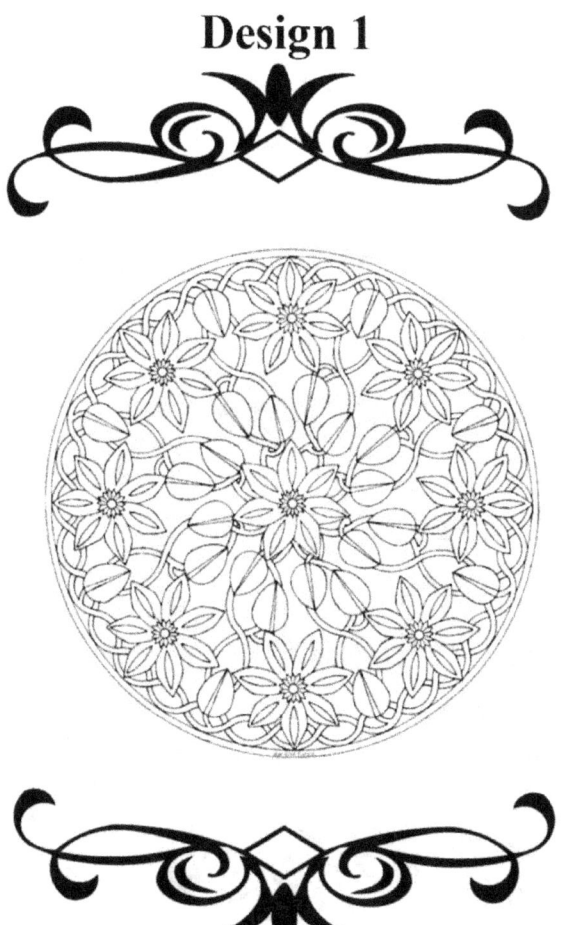

Design 2

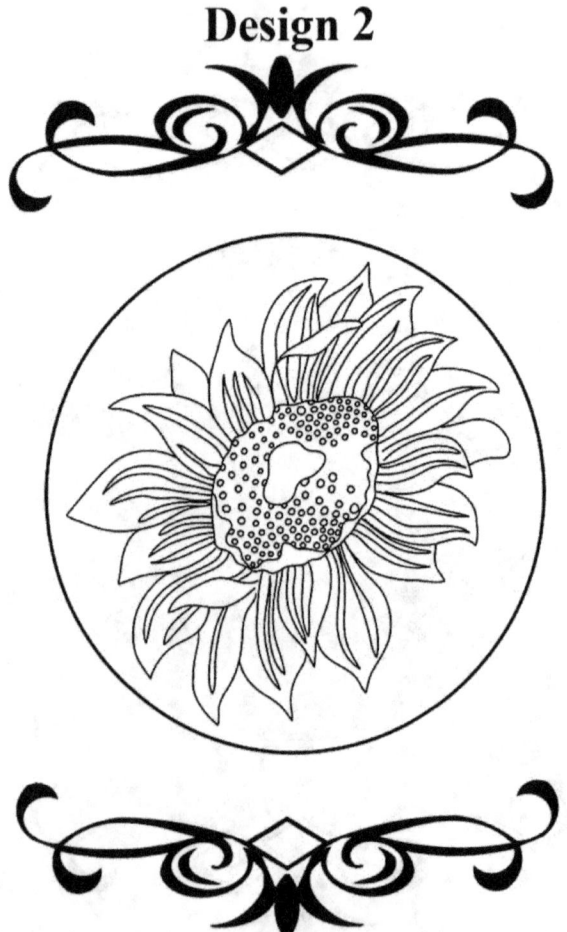

Design 3

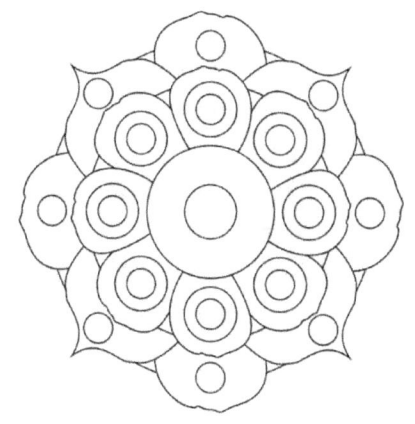

Design 4

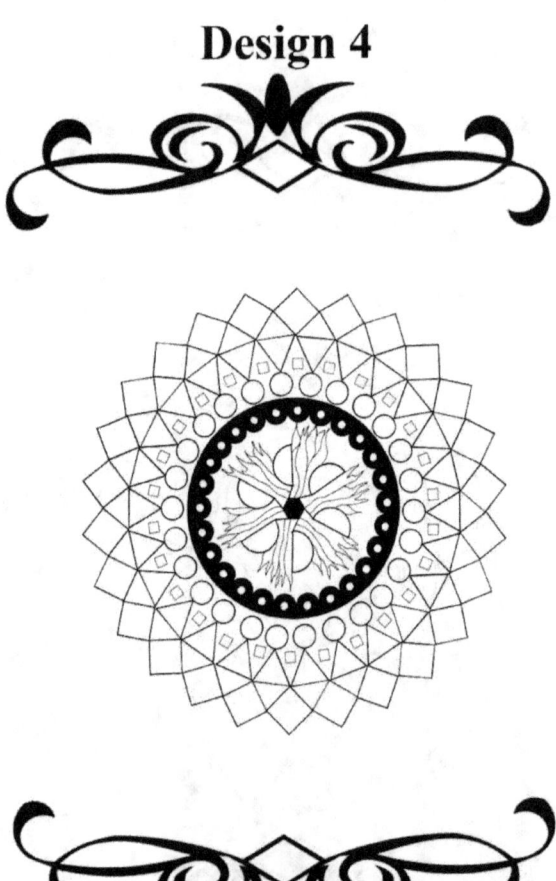

Design 5

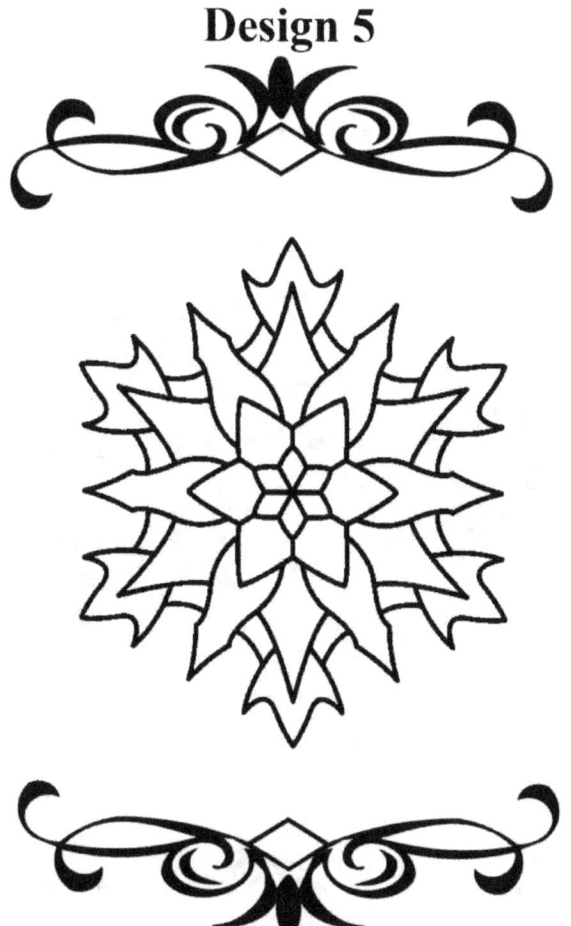

Design 6

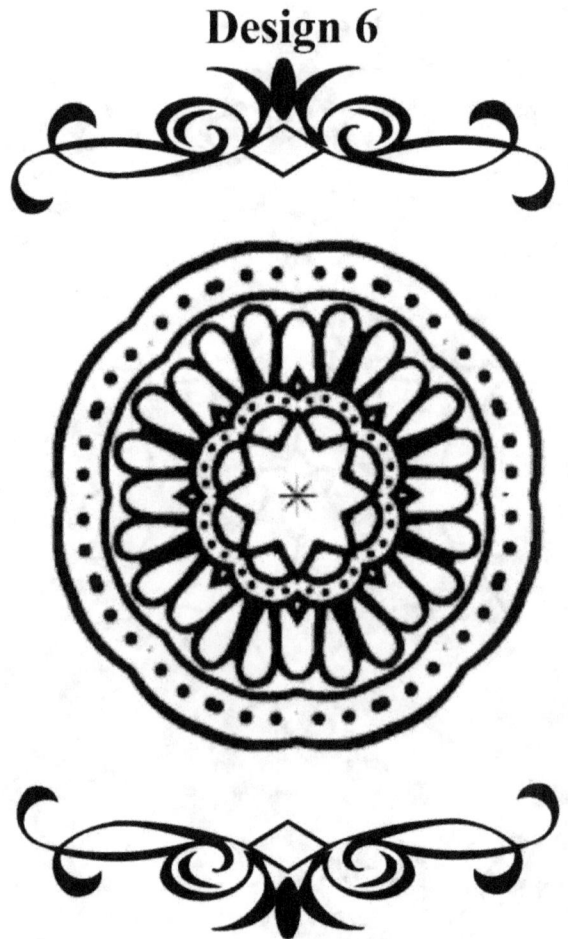

Design 7

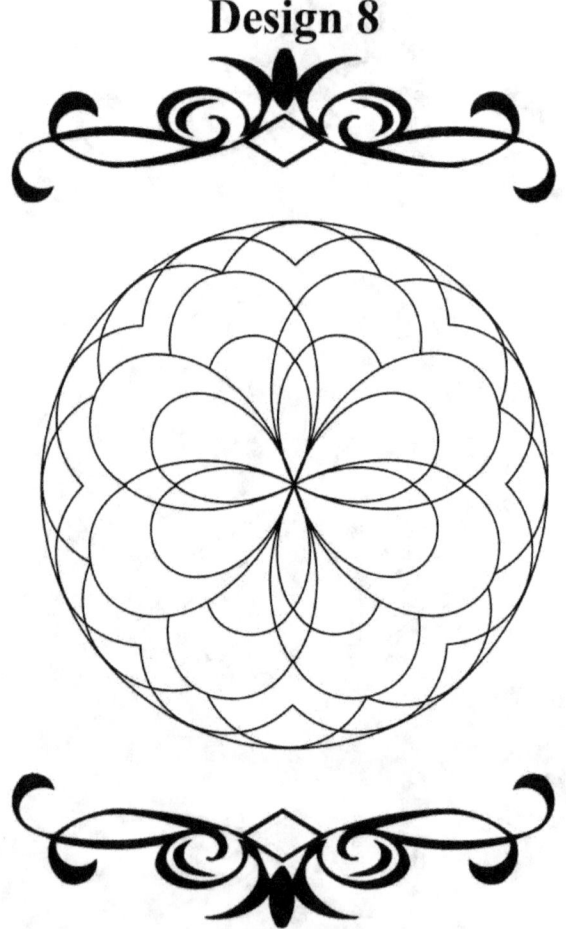

Design 8

Design 9

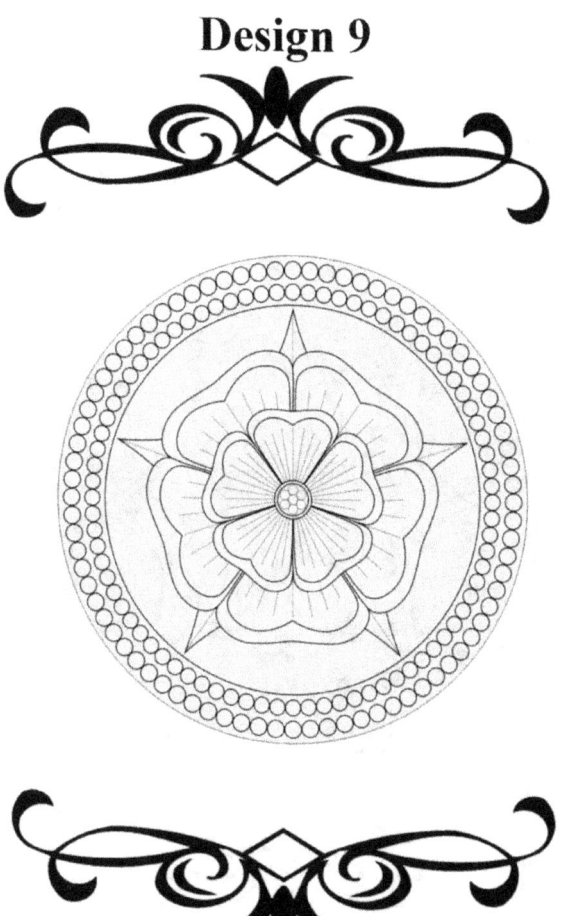

Design 10

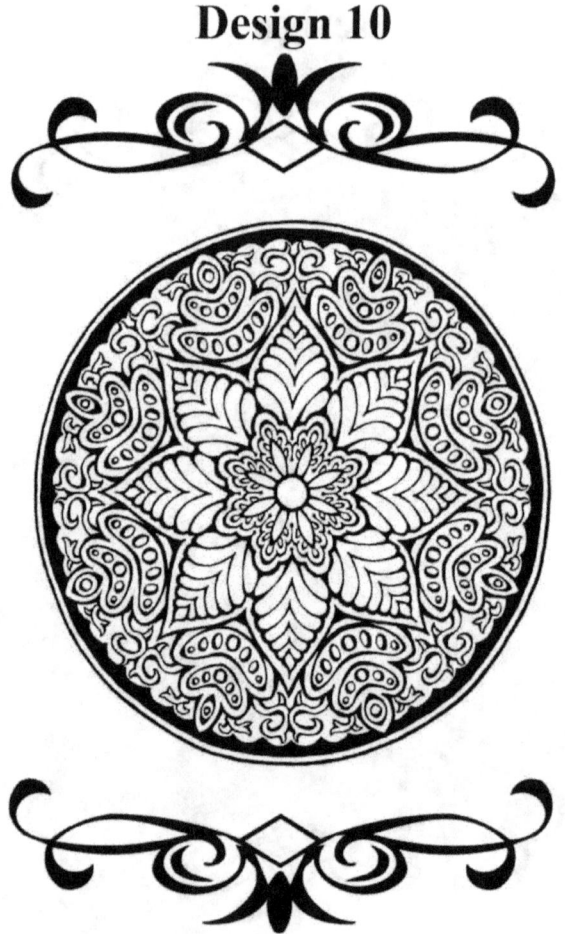

Design 11

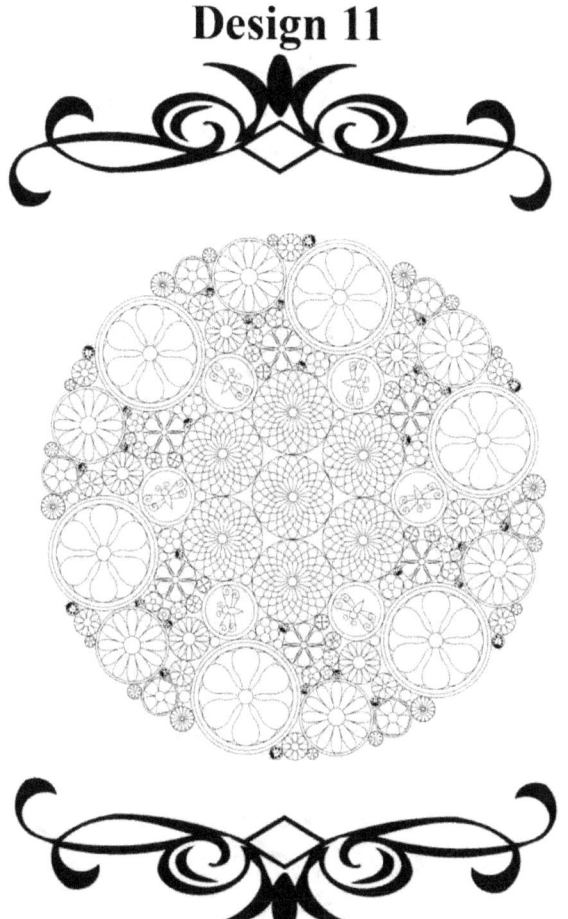

Design 12

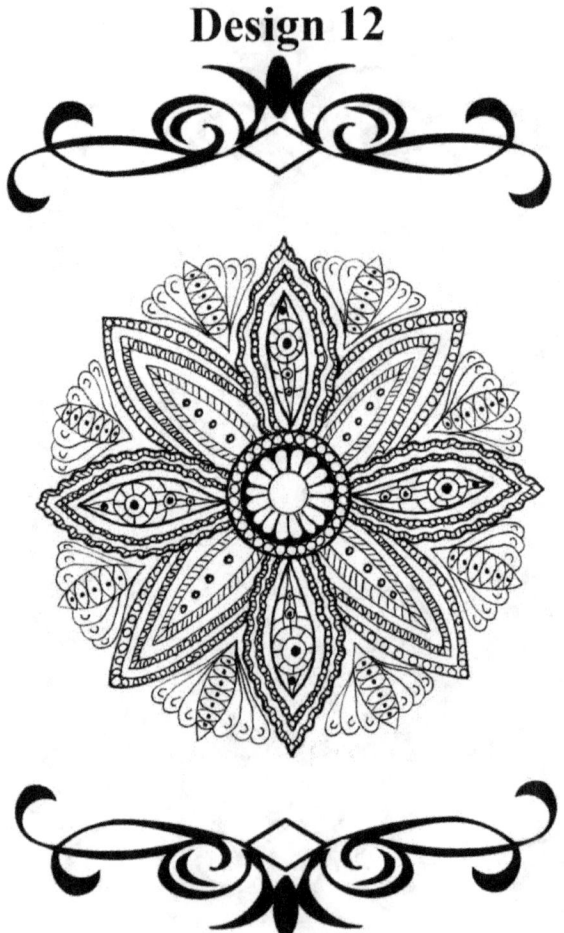

Design 13

Design 14

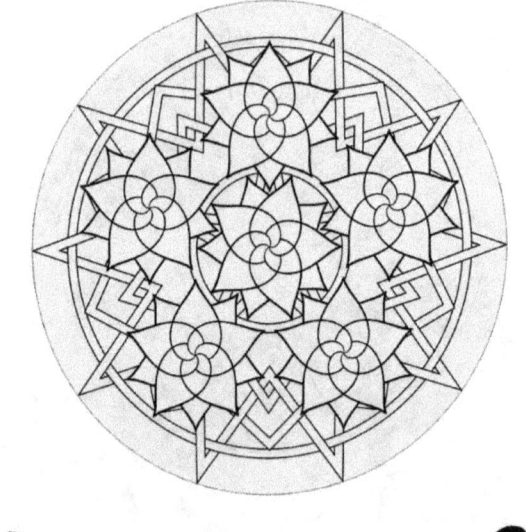

Design 15

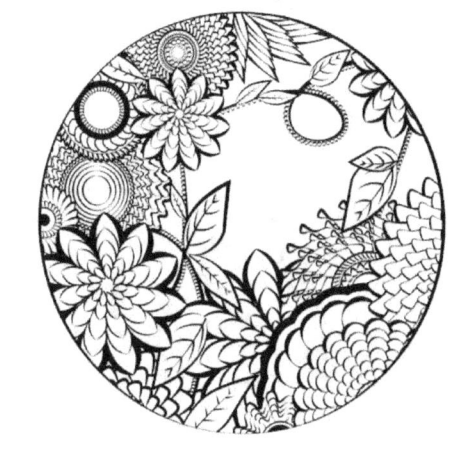

Design 16

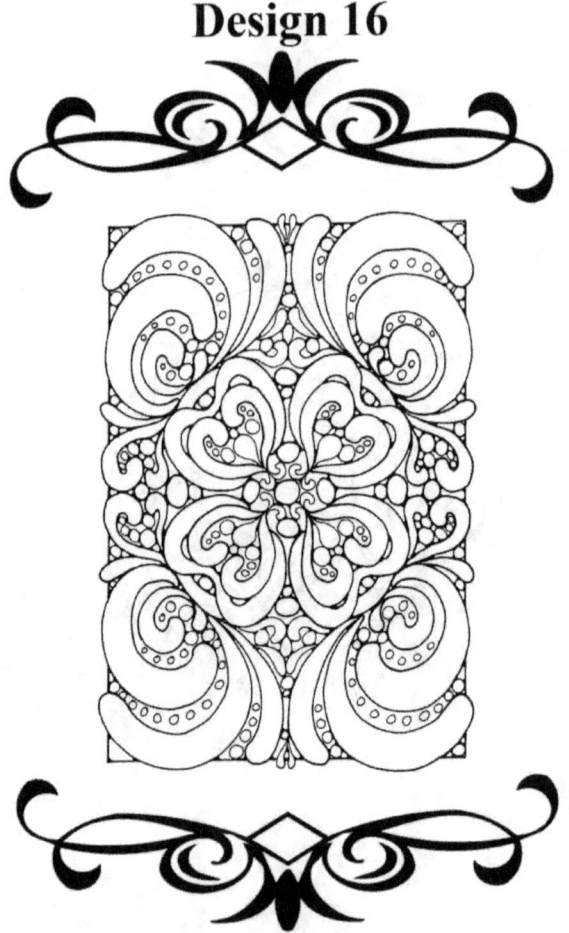

Design 17

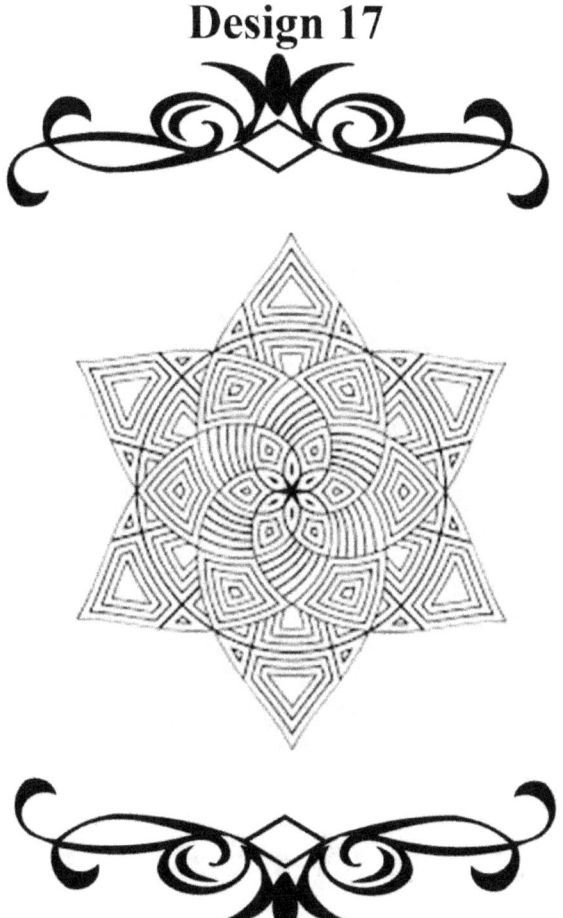

Design 18

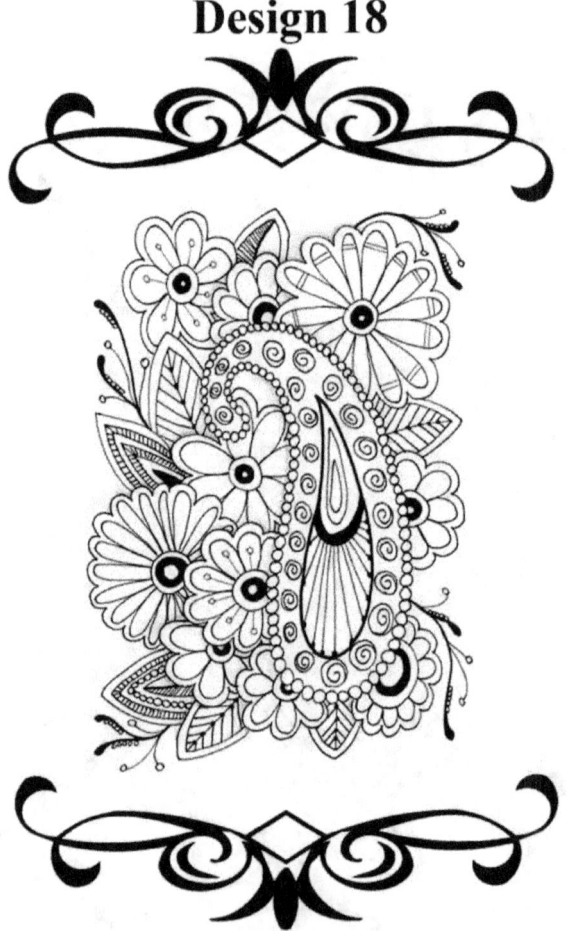

Design 19

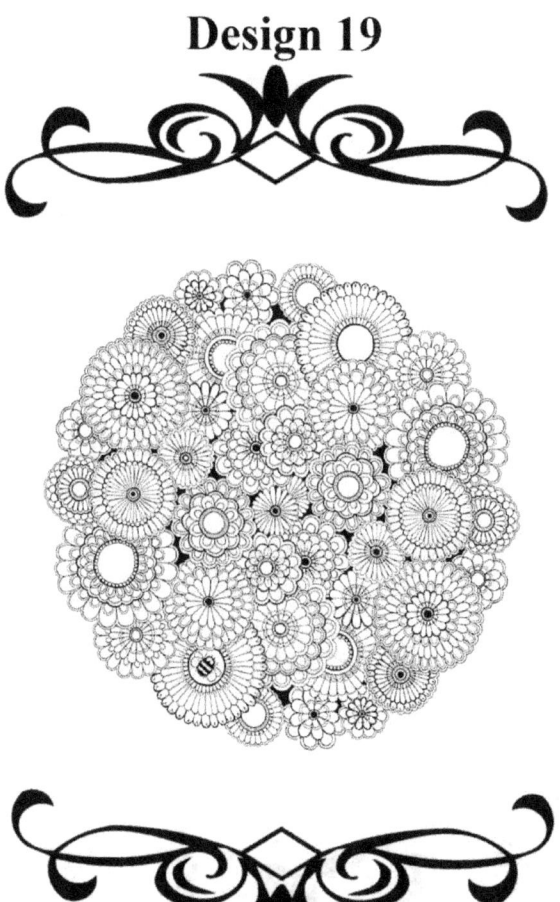

Design 20

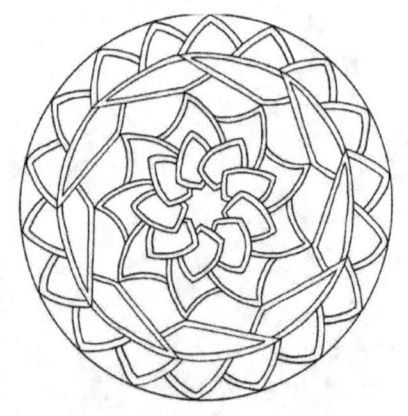

Design 21

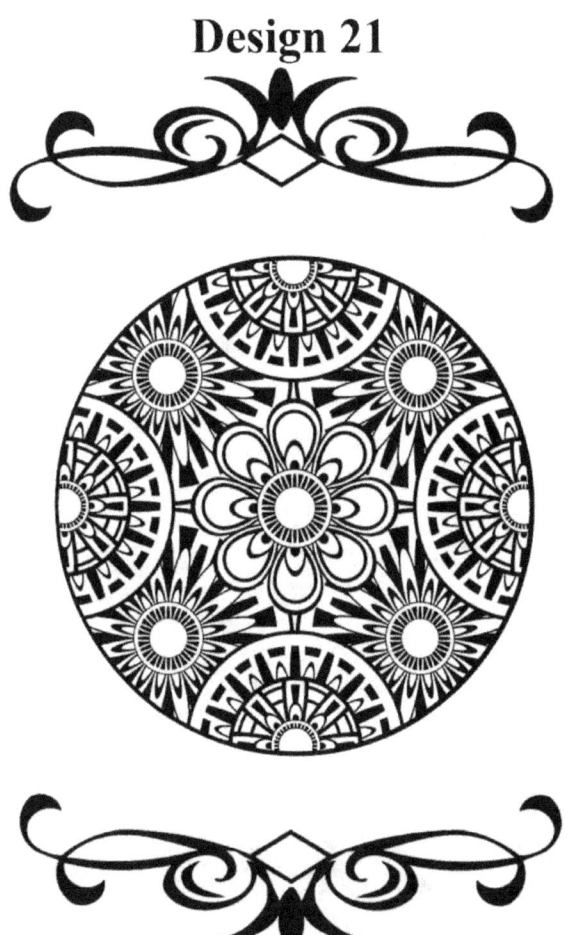

Design 22

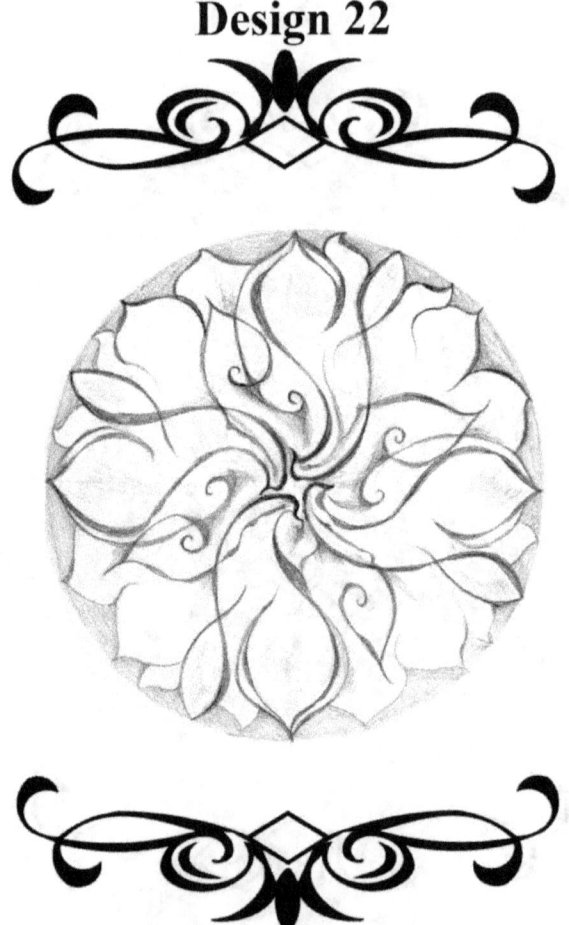

Design 23

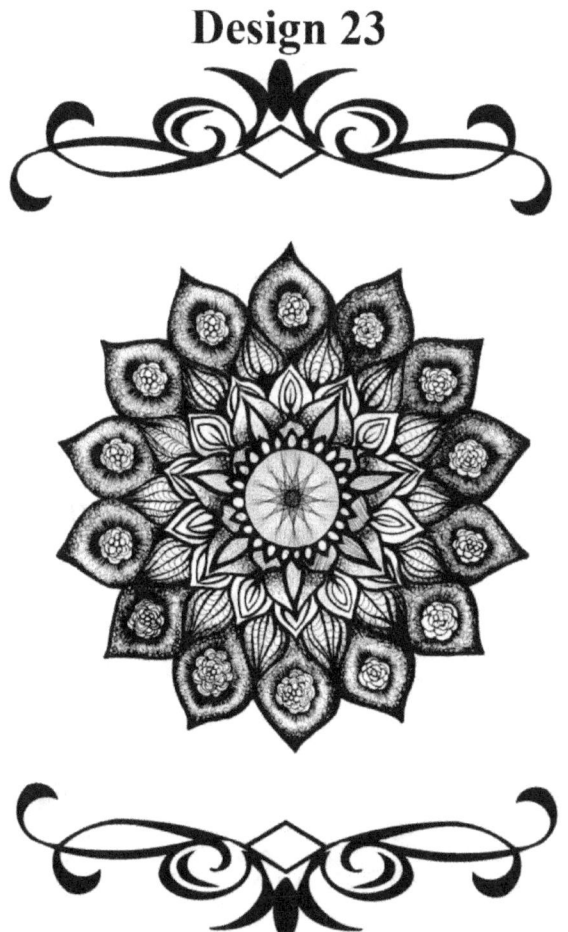

Design 24

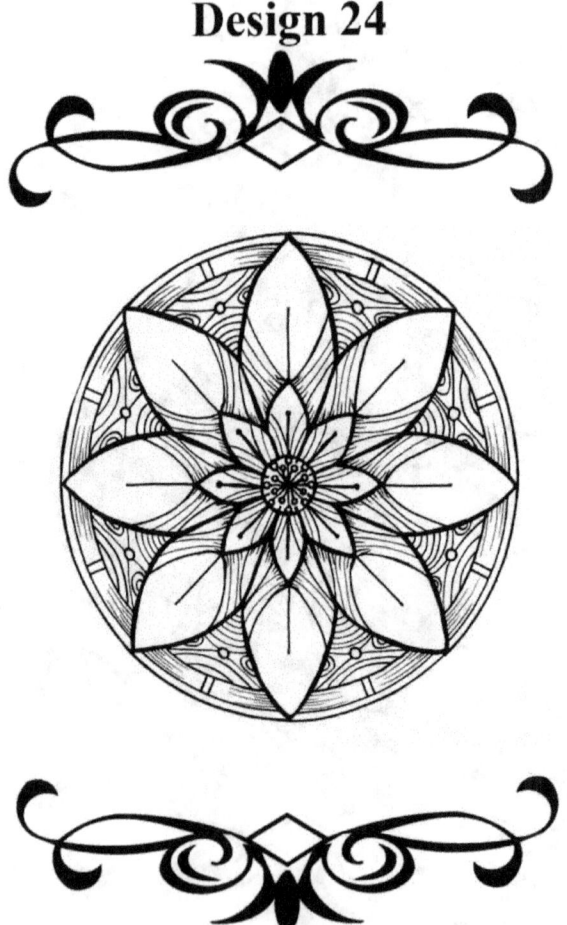

Design 25

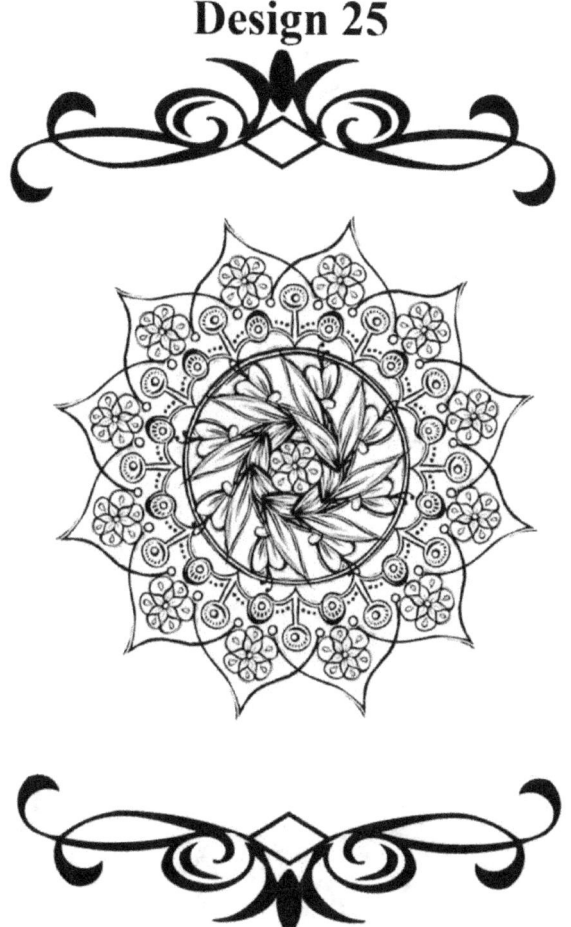

Design 26

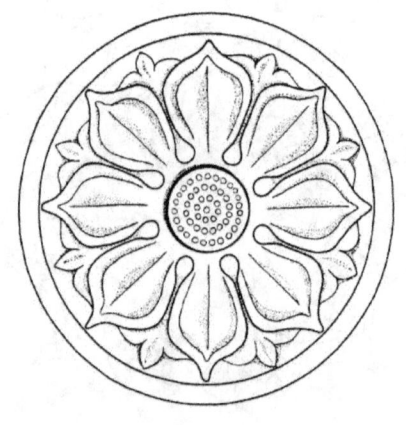

Design 27

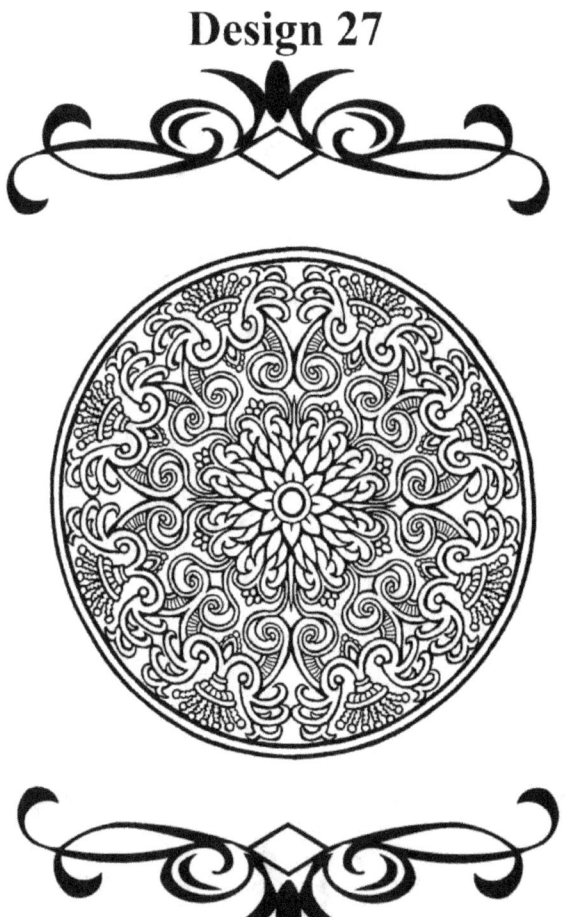

Design 28

Design 29

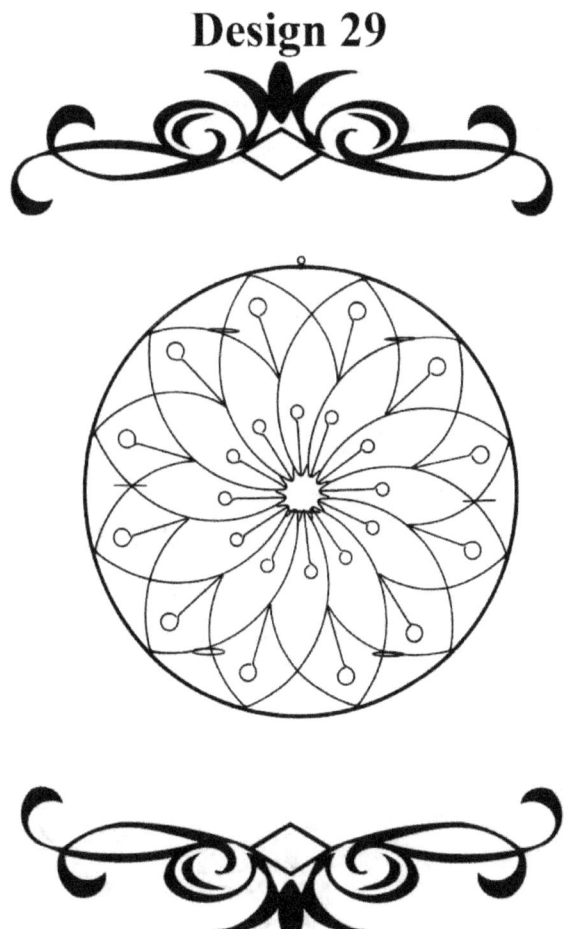

Design 30

www.ingramcontent.com/pod-product-compliance
Lightning Source LLC
Chambersburg PA
CBHW072030190526
45166CB00015B/1701